POCKET GUIDE TO
Flags

WILLIAM CRAMPTON

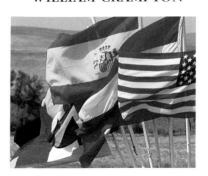

Shaker Heights High School Library

POCKET GUIDE TO
Flags

WILLIAM CRAMPTON

CANCELLED

CRESCENT BOOKS
New York • Avenel, New Jersey

929.9
Cra

©1992 Salamander Books Ltd.,
129-137 York Way,
London N7 9LG,
United Kingdom.

This 1993 edition published by Crescent Books,
distributed by Outlet Book Company, Inc.,
a Random House Company,
40 Engelhard Avenue,
Avenel,
New Jersey 07001

ISBN 0-517-08651-4

8 7 6 5 4 3 2 1

All rights reserved. No part of this book
may be reproduced, stored in a retrieval system
or transmitted in any form or by any means, electronic,
mechanical, photocopying, recording or otherwise without
the prior permission of Salamander Books Ltd.

All correspondence concerning the content of this
volume should be addressed to the publisher.

Credits
Editor: Bob Munro
Designer: Paul Johnson
Flag artworks: Mike Keep
Filmset: The Old Mill, London
Color reproduction: Regent Publishing Services Ltd.,
Hong Kong
Printed in Belgium by Proost International Book Production

The Author
Though he has a full-time career in adult education,
William Crampton is also the Director of the Flag
Institute, a research body interested in all aspects of the
world's flags past and present. His lifelong interest in the
subject now extends to flag design. Mr. Crampton lives
in Chester, Cheshire, England.

Picture Credits
Cover: Jeffrey M. Spielman/Image Bank UK; Endpapers:
TRH/E. Nevill; Page 1: TRH/E. Nevill; Pages 2-3: DOD;
Page 5: Marcel Isy-Schwart/Image Bank UK; Page 6:
Holger Schoenbeck/Image Bank UK; Page 7: Salamander
Books; Page 8: Marvin E. Newman/Image Bank UK:
Page 10: Salamander Books; Page 21: Salamander
Books; Page 34: John William Banagan/Image Bank UK;
Page 38: Salamander Books; Page 46: Salamander
Books; Page 52: Salamander Books.

Contents

Introduction

Flags are all around us everywhere today: national flags, local flags, commercial flags, flags on ships, flags on buildings, flags as stickers, flags as T-shirts. They are a quick, easy, and concise way of expressing ideas, of stating identity, of attracting attention and of enlivening the scene. Flags have been in use for centuries, some in the same form that we see today, but never so frequently. At one time they were the preserve of heraldry, or of the sailor, when they took the form of armorial banners or naval ensigns, but today they are used by everybody from the head of state, the government, the armed forces, to national institutions, voluntary organisations, sports clubs, yachtsmen and schools and colleges. The ones we see most frequently are national flags, the ones which represent a state or nation. With the many radical changes that have taken place in the last year or so, the number of national flags is now greater than ever before and keeping track of them is a full-time job as well as being a fascinating study. This book, being one of the latest available, will help to keep you up-to-date on the newest ones as well as providing a guide to the older ones.

National flags tend to follow a set form these days, unlike the wide panoply of patterns once in use. There is only one that is not rectangular in shape. Their designs fall into

Left: There are many ways to display flags. In this particular instance in a large atrium they have been flown vertically.

Below: Flags as national symbols have become ever more important over the centuries. Here at a summit meeting of NATO government heads, members' flags are flown in a show of unity.

Right: Flags are usually illustrated flying from left to right. The half of the flag nearest the flagstaff is known as the **hoist**. The outer half is the **fly**. By dividing the flag again, this time horizontally, the four quarters, or cantons, are obtained. The canton in the upper hoist position is known simply as **the canton**.

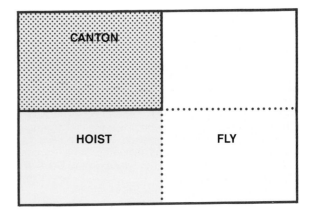

a number of distinct groups which make use of the various ways of dividing the rectangle: into horizontal or vertical stripes, into quarters (or *cantons*) or into a combination of stripes and a canton, as in the Stars and Stripes. They often contain distinctive emblems, such as the crescent and star symbolic of Islam, or patterns of stars such as the Southern Cross which is so frequent in the southern hemisphere.

Combinations of colours often show that countries wish to identify with each other, so that many African states use the combination red-yellow-green and perhaps also black, to proclaim a common background. Many countries which once looked to Russia for inspiration use red, white and blue, and many Arab states use red, white, black and green. Flags may also have common designs but in different colours, such as those of Scandinavian countries. This helps to explain why many national flags are at once distinctive and similar.

Left: Flags need not always be flown as a sign of aggressive nationalism — here they fly in peace at the Seville Expo, 1992.

Every country must have a national flag, and the new states which have emerged in the last year have, with a few exceptions, all taken steps to equip themselves with these essential attributes of nationhood, which they hoist at the United Nations, display at the Olympic Games, and exhibit in all sorts of ways to demonstrate their independence. Every state wants — by means of its flag — to say something about its nature, its aspirations, its affiliations and how it sees itself. By examining its national flag you discover get all these messages.

Part One: The Americas

Several countries in Central America use the blue and white colours of the United Provinces of Central America formed in 1823 after they had freed themselves from Mexico. The three republics in the north-west of the southern continent use colours derived from the flag of Francisco de Miranda, whilst in the River Plate region blue and white were also favoured, as symbolising the declaration of independence from Spain of 1810. Another 'Liberator' was José de San Martín who freed Chile and Peru from Spain. On the other hand the USA, which was the first American country to achieve independence, influenced the flag designs of many other states, including Cuba, Panama and Chile, which all have flags based on the Stars and Stripes of the United States.

ANTIGUA & BARBUDA

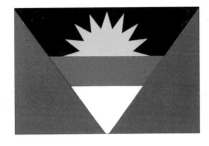

◁ **Capital:** St John's
Population: 85,000
This flag was adopted on 27 February 1967. The red field is for dynamism, whilst the V-shape stands for victory, within which is a simplified form of the devices in the national coat of arms.

▷ **Capital:** Buenos Aires
Population: 32,000,000
The flag represents the events of 25 May 1810 in Buenos Aires when the call went up for independence and the clouds drew back to reveal a blue sky. The flag was first used in this form on 12 February 1812.

ARGENTINA

BAHAMAS

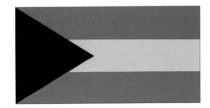

◁ **Capital:** Nassau
Population: 255,000
The colours of the national flag represent the vigour and unity of the inhabitants (the black triangle) and the golden sands and aquamarine waters of the islands. It was first flown at midnight on 9-10 July 1973.

▷ **Capital:** Bridgetown
Population: 300,000
The colours represent, like those of the Bahamas, the sea and the sands. The black trident recalls the old colonial badge of Barbados, and also symbolises the islanders' dependence on the sea.

BARBADOS

11

BELIZE

◁ **Capital:** Belmopan
Population: 190,000

The flag features the national coat of arms, which symbolises history and economy. They were first placed on a blue field in 1950 and revised at the time of independence in 1981, when the red stripes were added to the flag.

▷ **Capital:** La Paz
Population: 7,000,000

Bolivia has had a flag since 1825, but the present design dates from 30 November 1851 and is a simplification of the earlier forms. The state flag has the coat of arms in the centre of the yellow stripe.

BOLIVIA

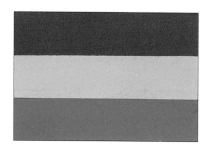

BRAZIL

◁ **Capital:** Brasilia
Population: 148,000,000

In 1889 the monarchy was overthrown and the imperial arms were replaced by a blue sphere, representing the night sky in Rio de Janeiro on 15 November 1889. The stars in the sky represent the federal states.

▷ **Capital:** Ottawa
Population: 26,850,000

The maple-leaf flag was adopted in 1965 after a very long period of controversy. The red and white are derived from the national coat of arms, and the maple-leaf is a long-standing emblem of Canada.

CANADA

CHILE

◁ **Capital:** Santiago
Population: 13,000,000

The Chilean flag is one of many heavily influenced by the Stars and Stripes. The colours are now said to stand for the struggle for independence (red), the blue of the sky and the snows of the Andes.

▷ **Capital:** Bogotá
Population: 32,000,000

The colours are derived from the flag of Miranda, first hoisted in 1806. This form, with the yellow of double width, was first used in 1819 by Greater Colombia, and re-adopted by the present state in 1861.

COLOMBIA

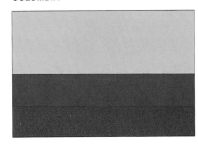

COSTA RICA

◁ **Capital:** San José
Population: 3,000,000

The flag is related to the blue and white flags of other central American states, with a red stripe added in 1848. The state flag has the arms on a white oval set near the hoist.

▷ **Capital:** Havana
Population: 10,600,000

This flag is modelled on the Stars and Stripes, and dates from 1848. It was adopted in Cuba on 20 May 1902. The five stripes stand for the five original provinces and the single star represents Cuba itself.

CUBA

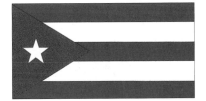

DOMINICA

◁ **Capital:** Roseau
Population: 87,000

The present flag is an adaptation of the one hoisted when the island became independent in 1878. The Sisserou parrot is indigenous to Dominica, and the ten stars stand for the ten parishes of the island.

▷ **Capital:** Santo Domingo
Population: 7,000,000

The flag is ultimately derived from that of Haiti which had conquered the east of the island, with a white cross laid over it and the blue and red parts re-arranged. The present design dates from 1844.

DOMINICAN REPUBLIC

ECUADOR

◁ **Capital:** Quito
Population: 10,500,000

The flag of Ecuador (which broke away from Colombia in 1830) can be distinguished from that of Colombia by its different proportions (1:2 as opposed to 2:3). As from 1900 the land flag has had the arms in the centre.

▷ **Capital:** San Salvador
Population: 5,300,000

The blue and white colours were first used in Central America in 1822, and have continued to be used by El Salvador. The plain flag is used only on land within the country; otherwise the arms appear in the centre.

EL SALVADOR

GRENADA

◁ **Capital:** St George's
Population: 100,000

The flag was adopted on independence on 7 February 1974, and features a nutmeg, the island's most lucrative product. The seven stars stand for the parishes, and the colours recall those of the Rastafarians.

▷ **Capital:** Guatemala
Population: 9,000,000

The flag is in the blue and white common to Central America, but arranged vertically, a design dating from 1871. The state flag has the arms in the centre, which feature a quetzal, Central America's most famous bird.

GUATEMALA

GUYANA

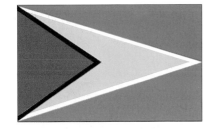

◁ **Capital:** Georgetown
Population: 800,000

The flag was adopted when the state became independent on 26 January 1966. It originated with a vexillologist, and was then processed by the College of Arms to arrive at the present design.

▷ **Capital:** Port-au-Prince
Population: 6,000,000

The flag is said to be derived from the *Tricolore* of France, which ruled the area until 1804, and originally had the colours arranged vertically. From 1964 until 1986 a rival flag, of red and black, was in use.

HAITI

HONDURAS

◁ **Capital:** Tegucigalpa
Population: 5,000,000
This flag is derived from that of the United
Provinces of Central America (see
El Salvador), and was adopted in 1866 when
the five stars (representing the original five
provinces) were added.

▷ **Capital:** Kingston
Population: 2,500,000
The flag was adopted in 1962. The design
originated in suggestions sent to a
parliamentary committee. They represent
natural wealth (gold), the hardships of the
past and the future (black), and agriculture.

JAMAICA

MEXICO

◁ **Capital:** Mexico City
Population: 84,000,000
This design dates from 1821. Found to be
similar to the Italian flag, the national arms
were placed in the centre. These are based
on the Aztec ideogram for the city of
Tenochtitlán (now Mexico City).

▷ **Capital:** Managua
Population: 3,700,000
The flag is almost identical to that of the
United Provinces of Central America, and
was adopted in this form in 1908. The arms
appear in the centre: their five volcanoes
represent the five original provinces.

NICARAGUA

16

PANAMA

◁ **Capital:** Panama City
Population: 2,500,000

The flag was introduced at the time the former Colombian province was seeking independence. It was designed by the first president, Manuel Amador Guerrero, and was first hoisted on 20 December 1903.

▷ **Capital:** Asunción
Population: 4,200,000

These colours appear on flags as early as 1812. The present design was adopted in 1842, and is unique among national flags in having a different emblem on each side: the obverse and reverse of the state seal.

PARAGUAY

PERU

◁ **Capital:** Lima
Population: 22,000,000

The colours of Peru were introduced by José de San Martín in 1820. The present design was adopted on 25 February 1825 and has remained unchanged since. The state flag has the arms in the centre.

▷ **Capital:** Basseterre
Population: 47,000

The flag was adopted on independence on 19 September 1983, and was the winning design in a competition. The two stars stand for hope and liberty, and the colours recall those of the Rastafarians.

ST. KITTS-NEVIS

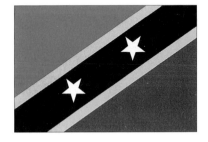

SAINT LUCIA

◁ **Capital:** Castries
Population: 150,000

The flag was adopted on 1 March 1967. The design represents the volcanic peaks of the Pitons above golden beaches amidst the blue sea. The black and white also represent the heritage of the people.

ST. VINCENT AND THE GRENADINES

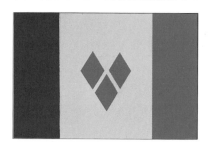

▷ **Capital:** Kingstown
Population: 110,000

The flag was revised on 12 October 1985 to include the three diamonds which represent the islands as the 'gems of the Antilles.' Previously the flag included the coat of arms set on a breadfruit leaf.

SURINAME

◁ **Capital:** Paramaribo
Population: 400,000

The flag was adopted on independence on 25 November 1975 and is said to be a combination of the colours of the political parties of that time. The gold star represents unity and hope for the future.

TRINIDAD AND TOBAGO

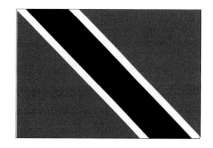

▷ **Capital:** Port-of-Spain
Population: 1,250,000

This flag also emerged from designs sent in by the public, and was adopted on independence. The colours are said to represent vitality (red), strength of purpose (black) and the surrounding sea (white).

UNITED STATES OF AMERICA

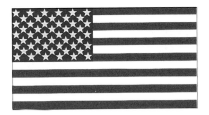

◁ **Capital:** Washington D.C.
Population: 250,000,000
The Stars and Stripes was adopted by
Congress on 14 June 1777. In 1818 it was
decided to keep to thirteen stripes and add
new stars for new states. The flag was last
altered on 4 July 1960.

▷ **Capital:** Montevideo
Population: 3,100,000
This flag is influenced both by the Stars and
Stripes and the colours of Argentina. The
present design was adopted on
independence on 11 July 1830. The nine
stripes represent the then nine departments.

URUGUAY

VENEZUELA

◁ **Capital:** Caracas
Population: 20,000,000
The present design dates from 20 April 1836.
The seven stars stand for the seven
provinces which supported the campaign for
independence and were placed in this form
in 1930.

Part Two: Europe

The political map of Europe has been re-drawn, and nowhere more so than in the former Union of Soviet Socialist Republics. After a long period of agitation the Baltic states resumed their independence at the time of the Moscow coup of 1991, and were soon joined by the Ukraine, Byelorussia and Moldavia. The Caucasus region saw the re-emergence of Georgia, Armenia and Azerbaijan, all now recognised as new sovereign states, despite the upheavals that have accompanied independence. In central Europe on the other hand the former state of East Germany gave way to a unified federal Germany, and Yugoslavia began to disintegrate. Two of its republics, Croatia and Slovenia have now become independent, and others may follow. This increases the number of sovereign states in Europe to forty two presenting a vast patchwork quilt of countries from Gibraltar to the Urals, all with their own characteristics and diverse national symbols.

ALBANIA

◁ **Capital:** Tirana
Population: 3,300,000
Although the communist regime is no more, the red star still appears above the traditional Byzantine eagle of Albania re-adopted in 1912. Additions have been made to the flag since, with the red star being added in 1946.

ANDORRA

▷ **Capital:** Andorra la Vella
Population: 51,400
The flag of Andorra is derived from the coat of arms, which includes quarters for places in both France and Spain. The country is ruled by the president of France and the Spanish bishop of Urgel.

ARMENIA

◁ **Capital:** Yerevan
Population: 3,288,000
The flag re-adopted in 1990 is like the one used in 1918-21 during the first period of independence. Designed by a heraldic commission, the colours are said to be those of the medieval kingdom of Armenia.

AUSTRIA

▷ **Capital:** Vienna
Population: 7,700,000
The red-white-red triband emerged as the national flag with the collapse of the Austro-Hungarian Empire in 1918, and survived the Nazi period of 1938-45. The colours are based on the arms of ancient Austria.

AZERBAIJAN

◁ **Capital:** Baku
Population: 7,038,000
The flag's red part represents the Azeris and their faith (Islam), the blue the skies and the green the land of Azerbaijan. The eight points of the star stand for the ethnic groups within the country.

BELGIUM

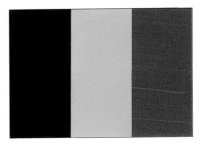

▷ **Capital:** Brussels
Population: 9,900,000
The colours of the Belgian flag are those of Brabant, and the format (adopted in 1831) that of the French tricolour. The flag for use at sea has the proportions 2:3 and for inland use 13:15.

BELORUS (Byelorussia)

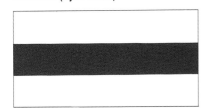

◁ **Capital:** Minsk
Population: 10,200,000
The flag is the same as that first used in March 1917 but suppressed two years later. The colours are derived from the coat of arms, which is essentially the same as that used by Lithuania.

BULGARIA

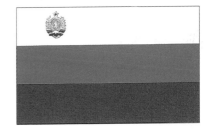

▷ **Capital:** Sofia
Population: 9,000,000
Like those of many other east European countries the flag of Bulgaria is based on that of Russia. During the communist regime the national emblem appeared in the white stripe near the hoist.

CROATIA

◁ **Capital:** Zagreb
Population: 4,660,000
The tricolour was adopted in 1848. During the communist regime a large red star was placed in the centre, but this was replaced in 1990. The five small shields represent different parts of the country.

CYPRUS

▷ **Capital:** Nicosia
Population: 700,000
The flag was adopted on independence in 1960 and is intended to be a symbol of peace between the rival communities. The emblem is a copper-coloured map of the island within a wreath of olive.

CZECHOSLOVAKIA

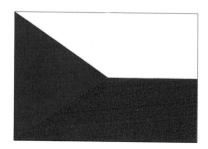

◁ **Capital:** Prague
Population: 15,700,000
Another flag based on the Pan-Slav or Russian colours, this one was adopted in 1920 for the first republic. Under the present constitution both the Czech and Slovak states have their own flags.

DENMARK

▷ **Capital:** Copenhagen
Population: 5,130,000
Thought to be the oldest national flag in continuous use. The arms of the cross were originally of equal length, but the outer one gradually became extended to form the typical Scandinavian cross.

ESTONIA

◁ **Capital:** Tallinn
Population: 1,570,000
The flag dates from 1881 and was used by the first republic in the period 1918-40. It was re-adopted in 1988, replacing the Soviet-style flag. The blue is the colour of the cornflower, Estonia's national flower.

FINLAND

▷ **Capital:** Helsinki
Population: 5,000,000
The blue and white colours date from the mid-nineteenth century and are said to stand for the lakes and snowfields of Finland. The present design was officially adopted in 1918.

FRANCE

◁ **Capital:** Paris
Population: 56,000,000
Known as the *tricolore*, the flag emerged from the Revolution of 1789, but with the colours in the reverse order. The present design dates from 1794, and has been in use continuously except for the period 1815-30.

GEORGIA

▷ **Capital:** Tbilisi
Population: 5,448,000
The cherry colour of the flag stands for joys past and present, the black for the period of Russian rule, and the white for hope for the future. The flag was first adopted in 1917, suppressed in 1921, and re-adopted in 1990.

GERMANY

◁ **Capital:** Berlin/Bonn
Population: 78,700,000

The German tricolour was officially adopted in 1848, suppressed in 1850, re-adopted in 1919, suppressed in 1933, and adopted once more in 1949. In 1990 it became the flag of a re-united Germany.

▷ **Capital:** Athens
Population: 10,000,000

The stripes on the Greek flag stand for the motto of the original freedom fighters: "Liberty or Death!" The colours derive from their flags, although the shade of blue has varied a lot over the years.

GREECE

HUNGARY

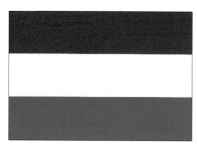

◁ **Capital:** Budapest
Population: 10,400,000

The colours are derived from the traditional coat of arms, which was restored in 1990. Hungary became independent in 1918, and re-adopted the tricolour first used in 1848. The flag lost its centre emblem in 1957.

▷ **Capital:** Reykjavik
Population: 258,000

The flag of Iceland is based on that of Norway (to which if once belonged) with the blue and red reversed. The flag dates from 1915 and became that of an independent republic in 1944.

ICELAND

IRELAND

◁ **Capital:** Dublin
Population: 3,600,000
The tricolour of Ireland is based on that of France, and dates from 1848. The colours stand for the Catholics and the Protestants (the 'Orangemen') and for peace between them. The flag was officially adopted in 1937.

▷ **Capital:** Rome
Population: 57,600,000
The Italian tricolour is also based on that of France, and dates from the French invasion under Napoleon in 1796. It was re-adopted in 1848 and became the flag of a united Italy in 1861.

ITALY

KAZAKHSTAN

◁ **Capital:** Alma-Ata
Population: 16,500,000
The former Soviet republic became independent on 16 December 1991 but has not yet adopted a new flag. It continues to fly the Soviet-style flag first introduced in 1953. However, a new design can be expected.

▷ **Capital:** Frunze
Population: 4,300,000
The flag depicts a bird's eye view of a yurt (a nomad's tent) in red in the centre of a gold sun, and was adopted on 3 March 1992. The former Soviet-style flag featured a broad horizontal blue and white stripe.

KYRGYZSTAN

LATVIA

◁ **Capital:** Riga
Population: 2,700,000

The Latvian flag was designed in 1917, based on the traditional colours of red and white, and was used by the first republic in the period 1918-40. It was re-adopted in 1990.

▷ **Capital:** Vaduz
Population: 30,000

Blue and red are the traditional colours of the principality, which was formed in 1719. The flag can often be seen hung vertically, in which case the blue strip and coronet are on the observer's left.

LIECHTENSTEIN

LITHUANIA

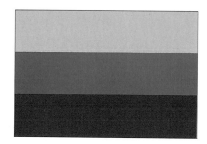

◁ **Capital:** Vilnius
Population: 3,690,000

The colours of Lithuania are not derived from the ancient coat of arms but were chosen by a heraldic commission in 1918. The flag was used until 1940, and re-adopted in 1988.

▷ **Capital:** Luxembourg
Population: 390,000

These colours are derived from the coat of arms, and are only coincidentally the same as those of the Netherlands. The flag in this form dates from 1848. A different flag is used by merchant ships.

LUXEMBOURG

MALTA

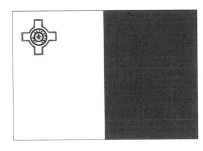

◁ **Capital:** Valetta
Population: 400,000

The emblem in the corner of the flag is the medal of the George Cross, awarded to the island in 1944. The colours of Malta are traditional ones, dating back to the days of the Knights of St John.

▷ **Capital:** Chisinau
Population: 4,340,000

The colours and eagle in the flag are derived from Romanian heraldry, whilst the bull's head is the special emblem of Moldavia. The flag dates from 1990, and is very similar to the pre-Communist flag of Romania.

MOLDOVA

MONACO

◁ **Capital:** Monaco-Ville
Population: 28,200

The colours are traditional ones of the Grimaldi family, who have ruled Monaco since 1297. The flag in this form dates from 1881, although red and white flags had been in use for centuries.

▷ **Capital:** The Hague
Population: 15,000,000

The Dutch colours are derived from those of the House of Orange, in that the upper stripe was originally orange. The orange-white-blue combination has been adopted in South Africa.

NETHERLANDS

NORWAY

◁ **Capital:** Oslo
Population: 4,250,000

The flag is an adaptation of that of Denmark (to which Norway belonged until 1814), designed in 1821. It did not become the flag of an independent Norway until 1905, when the country separated from Sweden.

▷ **Capital:** Warsaw
Population: 38,100,000

The Polish colours derive from the ancient coat of arms, restored in 1990. The present flag was adopted in 1919. During the communist period the eagle was deprived of its crown.

POLAND

PORTUGAL

◁ **Capital:** Lisbon
Population: 10,400,000

The historical flags of Portugal were blue and white, but red and green were instituted in the Revolution of 1910. Red is for revolution, and green for Portugal's achievements under King Henry the Navigator.

▷ **Capital:** Bucharest
Population: 23,300,000

The flag dates from 1848, and like many others is derived from the French tricolour. The colours are those of the arms of Wallachia and Moldavia, the two principal parts of the country.

ROMANIA

RUSSIAN FEDERATION

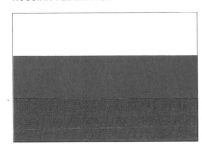

◁ **Capital:** Moscow
Population: 147,400,000
The colours are derived from those of the
Netherlands, and were instituted by Peter the
Great. The flag was officially adopted in
1799 but replaced by the Red Flag in 1917. It
was restored in August 1991.

▷ **Capital:** Ljubljana
Population: 1,950,000
The flag is the same as that of Russia, being
adopted in imitation in 1848. When Slovenia
was a communist republic in Yugoslavia the
flag had a red star over all, but the present
shield was substituted in June 1991.

SLOVENIA

SPAIN

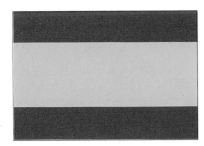

◁ **Capital:** Madrid
Population: 39,000,000
The present form of flag was adopted in 1785,
although with a crowned shield in the yellow
section. The flag was suppressed in 1931
and restored by Franco in 1939. Its colours
derive from the arms of Castile and of Aragon.

▷ **Capital:** Stockholm
Population: 8,500,000
The flag is in the Scandinavian cross
pattern, but the colours are taken from
the ancient arms of Sweden, three gold
crowns on blue. The flag dates back to at
least 1583.

SWEDEN

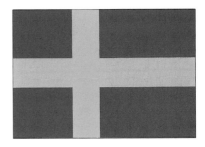

SWITZERLAND

◁ **Capital:** Bern
Population: 6,700,000
A white cross on red has signified
Switzerland since the Middle Ages, but the
flag was only made official in 1889. It seems
to derive from the arms of Schwyz, one of
the original three cantons of 1291.

▷ **Capital:** Dushanbe
Population: 5,110,000
This republic became independent with the
dissolution of the Soviet Union, but has not
yet adopted a new flag. The old flag, still in
use at the time of writing, was adopted on 20
March 1953.

TAJIKISTAN

TURKMENISTAN

◁ **Capital:** Ashkhabad
Population: 3,500,000
The flag depicts a length of carpet —
the country's most famous product — on
a field of green, and a crescent and five
stars. The flag was adopted on 19 February
1992.

▷ **Capital:** Ankara
Population: 53,000,000
Originally plain red, the flag acquired first a
crescent and then a star and was known in
this form from the eighteenth century. The
present layout was adopted in 1936, after the
abolition of the Caliphate.

TURKEY

UKRAINE

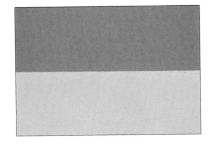

◁ **Capital:** Kiev
Population: 51,705,000
The flag dates back to 1848, and its colours are taken from the arms of Galicia, which now forms the western part of the country. It was used for the Ukrainian state of 1918-20, and was restored in September 1991.

UNITED KINGDOM

▷ **Capital:** London
Population: 57,300,000
The flag reflects the unions of England and Scotland and of Britain and Ireland in the three crosses representing the three countries. The present form dates from 1 January 1801.

UZBEKISTAN

◁ **Capital:** Tashkent
Population: 19,900,000
The new flag of the former Soviet Republic was adopted on 11 October 1991. The upper blue stripe recalls the flag of the famous emperor Tamerlane, and the 12 stars stand for the 12 months of the Moslem calendar.

YUGOSLAVIA

▷ **Capital:** Belgrade
Population: 10,469,000
The present flag dates from 1946, although the blue-white-red tricolour was instituted in 1919. Because of the violent situation in the former Yugoslav republic, only Serbia and Montenegro still use this today.

Part Three: Oceania

Many flags in the South Pacific area employ the Southern Cross constellation as an appropriate emblem, a practice which began in Australia. The area is also one where countries, often consisting of dozens of small islands spread over vast areas of sea, have been slow to achieve independence, and there are still many under the administration of France and the United States. Some were organised political states before being taken over by Europeans, and have symbols that go back to pre-colonial times.

Also in this region are states that still have flags based on the Union Jack: Australia and New Zealand, Fiji and Tuvalu. How long this will continue remains to be seen.

AUSTRALIA

◁ **Capital:** Canberra
Population: 17,000,000
The flag won a design competition in 1901
and was revised on 22 May 1909. The
Southern Cross is the badge of Victoria, the
large star is for the Australian commonwealth,
whilst the Union flag represents Britain.

▷ **Capital:** Suva
Population: 700,000
This design emerged from a design
competition held prior to independence in
1970. Although Fiji left the Commonwealth in
1987 the flag was not changed. However, a
new design may be adopted soon.

FIJI ISLANDS

KIRIBATI

◁ **Capital:** Bairiki
Population: 69,000
The flag is a banner of the arms, which
were granted to the then Gilbert and Ellice
Islands in 1937. The design depicts a
frigate bird flying over the sea before the
rising sun.

▷ **Capital:** Majuro
Population: 44,000
The flag was designed for the
autonomous republic set up in 1979. The
two stripes, represent the two chains of
islands, and the star their twenty four
municipalities.

MARSHALL ISLANDS

35

MICRONESIA

◁ **Capital:** Kolonia
Population: 105,000

This federation has recently become independent after a period of American rule. The four stars stand for the four states, set in the blue sea. This design dates from 1978 — before that there were six stars.

NEW ZEALAND

▷ **Capital:** Wellington
Population: 3,400,000

This flag evolved independently of that of Australia, and is in effect the old colonial ensign. The Southern Cross was adopted in New Zealand in 1869, and this flag was introduced in 1901, and confirmed in 1908.

PAPUA NEW GUINEA

◁ **Capital:** Port Moresby
Population: 3,800,000

This country was governed by Australia until 1975 when it gained independence. The bird of paradise dates from the earliest colonial times, and was combined with the Southern Cross in 1971.

SOLOMON ISLANDS

▷ **Capital:** Honiara
Population: 300,000

The five stars stand for the then five districts of the archipelago, and the design itself emerged from a design competition held prior to independence in 1978. The colours represent the nature of the country.

TONGA

◁ **Capital:** Nuku'alofa
Population: 100,000

The flag of Tonga dates from before the British Protectorate, having been adopted in 1874. The colours were also used in many other Polynesian island states in the nineteenth century.

▷ **Capital:** Funafuti
Population: 8,500

This flag was also the winning entry in a design competition: the array of stars represents the individual islands of the archipelago, and the general design may have been copied from that of Fiji.

TUVALU

VANUATU

◁ **Capital:** Port Vila
Population: 200,000

This flag was designed on the basis of the flag of the dominant political party, and dates from 5 March 1980. The device in the black triangle is a boar's tusk with two fern-fronds (representing wealth and peace).

▷ **Capital:** Apia
Population: 200,000

The flag is partly based on one used before 1899, but uses the Southern Cross borrowed from New Zealand, which ruled the islands until 1962. The extra small star was added to the design in 1949.

WESTERN SAMOA

Part Four: Central Asia and the Far East

Many Asian states have references to religious ideas in their flags, including the crescent and star of Islam, the wheel of Dharma of the Buddhists, and the sun of Japan. Others are purely political or refer to local 'specialities' such as the dragon of Bhutan. Like Africa, many countries of this region only regained or achieved independence in modern times. Some, however, such as Afghanistan, China, Thailand and Japan were never completely dominated by the Europeans. Their flags' histories go back much further in time. Mongolia and Korea had to free themselves from invasive neighbours. Both of these use another well-known Asian device, the *yin-yang* symbol, on their flags.

Flags

AFGHANISTAN

◁ **Capital:** Kabul
Population: 16,000,000
This country has had more flag changes
than any other, the latest in 1987. Its flag still
carries some old emblems: a wheat-sheaf, a
rising sun, and the pulpit and *mihrab* of a
mosque. The colours date back to 1928.

▷ **Capital:** Dhaka
Population: 110,000,000
The red disc originally had an outline map of
'Golden Bengal' in it, but this was dropped
in 1972, in order to simplify manufacture. The
red disc now stands for the revolution, and
the green for the green land.

BANGLADESH

BRUNEI

◁ **Capital:** Bandar Seri Begawan
Population: 300,000
The scroll was added to the original plain
flag in 1959; the flag dates from 1906 when
the white and black stripes were added. The
whole represents the state supported by the
Sultan and his two chief ministers.

▷ **Capital:** Beijing
Population: 1,100,000,000
Red is the Chinese colour, as well as
being the colour of communism. The
design was adopted at the inauguration
of the People's Republic on 1 October
1949.

CHINA

HONG KONG

◁ **Capital:** Victoria
Population: 5,800,000
Whilst it is still a British colony Hong Kong continues to use a British Blue Ensign with the badge in the fly. A flag for use after reunion with China has also been chosen, of red with a white flower in the centre.

▷ **Capital:** New Delhi
Population: 850,000,000
At the centre of the Indian flag is the Chakra, the Wheel of Dharma, which was added to the flag at the time of independence in 1947. The basic design of the flag was originally that of the Indian Congress Party.

INDIA

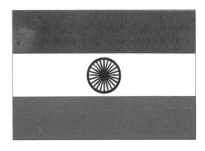

INDONESIA

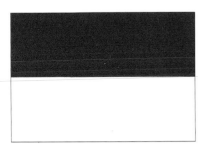

◁ **Capital:** Jakarta
Population: 177,000,000
The flag dates from the time of the independence movement. It was first hoisted in 1945, and then officially adopted on 27 January 1949. The colours are said to be those of the pre-Islamic empire of Majapahit.

▷ **Capital:** Tokyo
Population: 123,000,000
The Japanese flag is known as the *Hi-No-Maru* or 'Sun-Disc Flag', and was adopted as the national flag in 1870. Its design commemorates the legendary descent of the Emperors from the sun goddess.

JAPAN

KAMPUCHEA

◁ **Capital:** Phnom Penh
Population: 7,700,000
The government flag of Kampuchea is red over blue with a gold outline of the temple of Angkor Wat in the centre (the temple has always been the emblem of Kampuchea).

▷ **Capital:** Pyongyang
Population: 21,800,000
The flag of the People's Republic was adopted in 1948, when the country was partitioned. The colours of the flag are like those of the rival regime in the south, but here have a distinctly communistic style.

KOREA (NORTH)

KOREA (SOUTH)

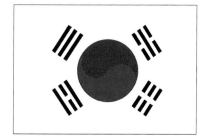

◁ **Capital:** Seoul
Population: 42,500,000
The flag is based on that of the old kingdom of Korea prior to 1910. The device is the *yin-yang* symbol surrounded by the four major characters from the *I Chi* book of divination. The flag was adopted on 25 January 1950.

▷ **Capital:** Vientiane
Population: 4,000,000
The national flag was originally the party flag of the *Pathet Lao* movement, which took control of the country in November 1975. The white disc is said to represent the promise for a bright new future.

LAOS

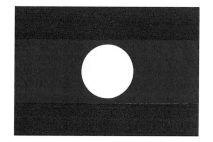

MALAYSIA

◁ **Capital:** Kuala Lumpur
Population: 17,500,000
The flag is an adaptation of the one introduced for the Malayan Federation in 1950, with extra stripes and points of the star being added for the new members who joined in 1963.

▷ **Capital:** Malé
Population: 200,000
The national flag was originally the civil ensign of the Maldive Sultanate. The red field recalls the fact that the islands were colonised by Oman; the green panel was added to this in the 1930s.

MALDIVE ISLANDS

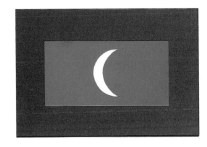

MONGOLIA

◁ **Capital:** Ulan Bator
Population: 2,100,000
The device on the flag of Mongolia is the *soyonbo*, a combination of mystical elements. From 1940-1992 the emblem was topped by a yellow star, which was removed when the new constitution was adopted in 1992.

▷ **Capital:** Yangon
Population: 41,000,000
The first flag of Burma (as it was known) was adopted in 1948. The present emblem was placed in the canton in 1974. The fourteen stars stand for the seven states and the seven divisions of the country.

MYANMAR

NEPAL

◁ **Capital:** Katmandu
Population: 19,500,000
The only national flag that is not a rectangle; it was originally two separate pennants. The sun and moon are traditional symbols, and the dark red represents the rhododendron, the country's national flower.

▷ **Capital:** Islamabad
Population: 110,000,000
The flag is derived from the party flag of the Moslem League, which led the country to independence in 1947. The white vertical stripe was added in 1947 to represent religious and racial minorities.

PAKISTAN

PHILIPPINES

◁ **Capital:** Manila
Population: 60,000,000
The Philippine flag was designed by nationalists living in exile during Spanish rule. It was used again during the American and Japanese occupations, and adopted as the flag of independent republic in 1946.

▷ **Capital:** Singapore
Population: 2,700,000
The five stars in the flag of Singapore stand for democracy, peace, progress, justice and equality, but the crescent moon does not just represent Islam. The flag was introduced on 3 December 1959.

SINGAPORE

SRI LANKA

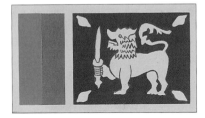

◁ **Capital:** Colombo
Population: 17,000,000

The original flag, adopted in 1948 had the lion and sword only, and had originally been the flag of a Ceylonese kingdom, Kandy. In 1951 the green and orange strips were added to represent the Moslems and Tamils.

▷ **Capital:** Taipei
Population: 20,000,000

The flag used in Taiwan is the same as that of the Chinese Republic, adopted in 1928, itself based on the flag of the *Kuomintang*, which was the dominant party in China until 1949. In 1950 the republic re-formed on Taiwan.

TAIWAN

THAILAND

◁ **Capital:** Bangkok
Population: 56,000,000

The Thai flag developed out of several previous models and assumed its present form in 1917. The flag was made red, white and blue to express solidarity with the Allies in World War I.

▷ **Capital:** Hanoi
Population: 63,000,000

The flag is the same as that of North Vietnam, and became that of the whole country on 2 July 1976. It has the same origins as that of China, ie in the communist and nationalist movements at the time of foreign occupation.

VIETNAM

Part Five: North Africa and the Middle East

This predominantly Moslem part of the world has flags with many features in common: the crescent and star of Islam, used originally by the Ottoman empire, the black, white, red and green of the Pan-Arab colours, derived from the flag used by Sherif Husain in the First World War, which lives on in Jordan, Palestine, Kuwait and the UAE; the red, white and black instituted by Colonel Nasser in 1952 (still used in Egypt, Syria, Sudan, Iraq and other countries once linked with Egypt); the red and white of the Persian gulf states; and other references to Islam as in the flags of Saudi Arabia and Iran. Exceptions are the plain flag of Libya and the blue and white of Israel.

ALGERIA

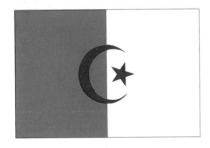

◁ **Capital:** Algiers
Population: 25,000,000

The flag was adopted by the liberation movement in 1954. It became the symbol of independent Algeria in 1962. The crescent and star have an unusual shape indicating wealth and increase.

▷ **Capital:** Manama
Population: 690,000

One of several Gulf States' flags in red and white, this unusual form with a serrated dividing line was introduced in 1932; perhaps to distinguish it from those of its neighbours in what is now the United Arab Emirates.

BAHREIN

EGYPT

◁ **Capital:** Cairo
Population: 54,000,000

The colours were introduced in 1952, as was the eagle of Saladin badge. The present form, with the arms all in gold in the centre, was adopted in 1984. Previous flags had a gold hawk (1971-84) and two green stars (1958-71).

▷ **Capital:** Tehran
Population: 55,000,000

Allahu Akbar ("Allah is Great") is the inscription, repeated twenty two times, along the edges of the green and red stripes, added in 1980 to the flag of Iran. In the centre is an emblem combining several Islamic concepts.

IRAN

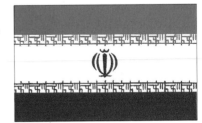

IRAQ

◁ **Capital:** Baghdad
Population: 17,100,000
The same inscription appears on the flag of Iraq. Previously the flag was like the former flag of Egypt but with three green stars, a form adopted in 1963 when a possible union with Egypt and Syria was in prospect.

▷ **Capital:** Jerusalem/Tel Aviv
Population: 4,700,000
The only non-Islamic state in the region has a flag based on the tokens of the Jewish faith, the star of David and the blue and white of the prayer shawl. The basic design dates from at least 1885.

ISRAEL

JORDAN

◁ **Capital:** Amman
Population: 3,100,000
This flag is very similar to the one used in the revolt led by the present king's ancestor, the Sherif of Mecca. The white star was added in 1928 at a time when Iraq had a very similar flag.

▷ **Capital:** Kuwait
Population: 1,500,000
This flag is also in the Pan-Arab colours, and was adopted in 1961, when the state resumed its independence. Prior to that the flag was red with a white inscription, like those of other Persian Gulf states.

KUWAIT

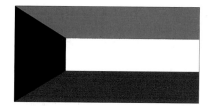

LEBANON

◁ **Capital:** Beirut
Population: 3,000,000

The cedar of Lebanon is an ancient badge of the area, and was added to the flag in 1943. The red and white colours are said to stand for the old ruling clans.

LIBYA

▷ **Capital:** Tripoli
Population: 4,200,000

Libya has also had several flags since independence in 1951, sharing a flag with Egypt in the period 1971-77. The present flag was introduced following the break with Egypt in 1977.

MAURITANIA

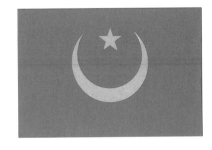

◁ **Capital:** Nouakchott
Population: 2,000,000

The simple flag of Mauritania represents the idea of the country as an Islamic Republic, and was introduced in 1959. Here the crescent and star are quite different from those of neighbouring Algeria.

MOROCCO

▷ **Capital:** Rabat
Population: 24,000,000

The flag of Morocco was originally plain red, indicating the Sultan's alleged descent from the Prophet (like the Sherif of Mecca). The green pentangle, or Solomon's Seal, was added in 1917.

49

94 8907

Flags

OMAN

◁ **Capital:** Muscat
Population: 1,400,000

The flag of Oman was also originally plain red (like those of other states in the area). The present design was introduced in 1970. The device in the canton consists of two swords, a dagger and a horse-bit.

QATAR

▷ **Capital:** Doha
Population: 500,000

Also originally plain red, the flag has acquired a serrated section like that of Bahrein, and an unusual red colour, as well as unusual proportions (11:28). These all help to distinguish it from similar flags of the region.

SAUDI ARABIA

◁ **Capital:** Riyadh
Population: 15,000,000

The inscription is the Islamic creed, "There is no God but Allah and Mohammed is the Prophet of Allah". The sword represents the ruling Saudi dynasty and was added in 1902.

SUDAN

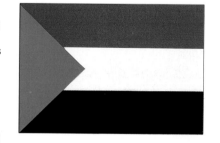

▷ **Capital:** Khartoum
Population: 25,500,000

Another flag in the Pan-Arab colours, but in an arrangement very like the flag of Egypt, adopted in 1970. The same colours are used by the *Umma*, the political descendents of the Mahdi.

50

SYRIA

◁ **Capital:** Damascus
Population: 12,000,000
The flag is identical with the flag of the
United Arab Republic (Egypt and Syria) of
1958-62, which was re-adopted in 1980. Syria
has had many changes of flag, and also
shared a flag with Iraq and Egypt.

▷ **Capital:** Tunis
Population: 8,000,000
This flag is derived from that of Turkey, and
was created about 1835. It has remained in
use ever since, during the many changes of
regime. The crescent and star are similar to
those on the flag of neighbouring Algeria.

TUNISIA

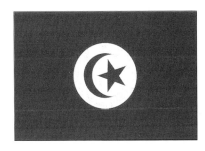

UNITED ARAB EMIRATES

◁ **Capital:** Abu Dhabi
Population: 2,000,000
The emirates first became a federation in
1968 when their flag was white with red
bands and a green star. Since independence,
the flag has featured the Pan-Arab colours
with the traditional colour red in the hoist.

▷ **Capital:** San'a
Population: 11,000,000
Yemen was re-united in 1990. The two
previous states both had flags of red, white,
black and so a plain flag in these colours
(originally derived from Egypt) was adopted
for the new united state.

YEMEN

Part Six: Sub-Saharan Africa

Ghana was the first country in sub-Saharan Africa to achieve independence from European rule, whilst Ethiopia and Liberia were never colonised in this sense (apart from Italy's occupation of Ethiopia, 1936-41). Ghana's leader, Kwame Nkrumah, was heavily influenced by a Jamaican negro activist, Marcus Garvey, who in the 1920s and 30s promoted the idea of emancipated American negroes returning to Africa. Garvey was also respected by the Rastafarians, a cult that arose in Jamaica following the coronation of Ras Tafara as Emperor of Ethiopia in 1931. The 'Rastas' adopted the colours of the flag of Ethiopia (green, yellow, red) and combined them with Garvey's 'Back to Africa' flag of black, red and green. Garvey also invented the Black Star emblem, which is now found on many African flags, the first being that of Ghana in 1957.

ANGOLA

◁ **Capital:** Luanda
Population: 9,000,000
The flag was adopted on independence in
1975 and was based on the flag of the MPLA
liberation movement. The colours stand for
the African continent (black), the blood shed,
and the riches of the country.

▷ **Capital:** Porto Novo
Population: 4,600,000
The flag was adopted in 1959, prior to
independence, but was replaced in 1975 with
a green flag with a red star when the
country's name was altered. The original flag
was restored on 1 August 1990.

BENIN

BOTSWANA

◁ **Capital:** Gaborone
Population: 1,200,000
The flag was adopted on independence in
1966. The basic blue colour stands for water
and its importance to the country, whilst the
black and white represent the ethnic groups
in the population.

▷ **Capital:** Ouagadougou
Population: 9,000,000
Originally known as Upper Volta, the country
adopted its present name and flag in August
1984. The previous flag was a horizontal
tricolour of black, white and red, but the
present one employs Pan-African colours.

BURKINA FASO

53

BURUNDI

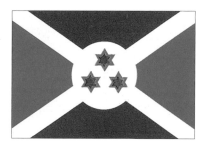

◁ **Capital:** Bujumbura
Population: 5,500,000

The basic design of the flag dates back to independence in 1962 but the central emblem has altered twice since then. The three stars represent the three ethnic groups of the country and were added in 1967.

CAMEROON

▷ **Capital:** Yaondé
Population: 11,200,000

Cameroon's basic flag was adopted in 1957 but has been altered twice since then. The present design, with a single central star, was introduced on 20 May 1975. The colours are the Pan-African ones.

CAPE VERDE ISLANDS

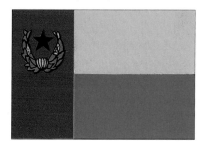

◁ **Capital:** Praia
Population: 400,000

The flag design derives from the flag of the nationalist movement which liberated these islands and Portuguese Guinea. This flag is distinguished from that of Guinea-Bissau by the wreath around the star.

CENTRAL AFRICAN REPUBLIC

▷ **Capital:** Bangui
Population: 3,000,000

This flag combines the Pan-African colours with those of France, which once ruled the area, and was adopted in 1958. The gold star stands for the political ideals of the time of independence.

CHAD

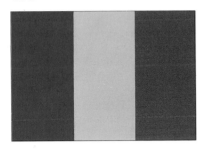

◁ **Capital:** N'Djamena
Population: 5,400,000

This is another combination of the Pan-African and French colours, and was introduced in 1959. The basic flag is identical to that of Romania, and is very similar to the flag of Andorra.

COMOROS

▷ **Capital:** Moroni
Population: 500,000

The four stars stand for the four main islands. This design was introduced in 1978 following a change of government, although the idea of the crescent and four stars goes back to 1963.

CONGO

◁ **Capital:** Brazzaville
Population: 2,300,000

The flag in the Pan-African colours was first adopted on 18 August 1959 but was replaced in January 1970 with a red flag with a green and gold emblem in the canton. The original flag was restored on 10 June 1991.

CÔTE D'IVOIRE

▷ **Capital:** Yamoussoukro (Abidjan)
Population: 12,000,000

The flag of orange-white-green was introduced in 1959, prior to independence, and has remained in use ever since. It has the colours in the opposite order to those of Ireland, and also has different proportions.

DJIBOUTI

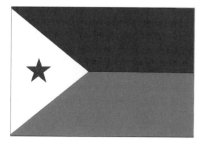

◁ **Capital:** Djibouti
Population: 490,000

The flag is based on that of the dominant political party at the time of independence. The blue represents the Issas, who are related to the Somalis, and the green part the Afars. The red star represents unity.

▷ **Capital:** Malabo
Population: 420,000

This flag was introduced on independence in 1968. The arms contain six stars to represent the six parts of the country. The blue triangle stands for the sea that unites all the different parts.

EQUATORIAL GUINEA

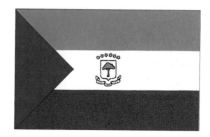

ETHIOPIA

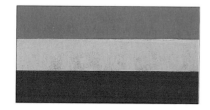

◁ **Capital:** Addis Ababa
Population: 49,000,000

The colours are the inspiration of the Rastafarian and Pan-African colours. The flag dates from 1897 and has remained in use ever since. The state flag has the arms in the centre, but new ones are awaited.

▷ **Capital:** Libreville
Population: 1,200,000

The flag represents another version of the combination of French and Pan-African colours, and dates from 9 August 1960. Although officially in the proportions 3:4 in practice it is of normal shape.

GABON

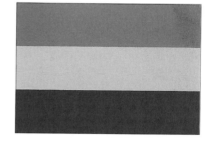

56

GAMBIA

◁ **Capital:** Banjul
Population: 850,000
One African flag that is not political in origin.
It was designed by a Gambian and
represents the blue Gambia river flowing
through the country. It dates from 18
February 1965, the day of independence.

GHANA

▷ **Capital:** Accra
Population: 14,000,000
The first 'new' African state, Ghana was also
the first country to use the Pan-African
colours derived from those of Ethiopia and
from Marcus Garvey's 'back to Africa'
movement.

GUINEA

◁ **Capital:** Conakry
Population: 7,000,000
Guinea has also borrowed the Ethiopian
colours, here arranged vertically, like the
French *Tricolore*, and adopted on 10
November, 1958. The flag should not be
confused with that of Mali.

GUINEA-BISSAU

▷ **Capital:** Bissau
Population: 1,000,000
This former Portuguese colony was linked in
the independence struggle with Cape Verde,
and so has a very similar flag. In this case
the flag has the proportions 1:2 and a black
star only on the red stripe.

KENYA

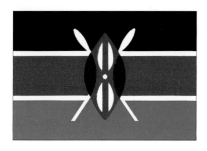

◁ **Capital:** Nairobi
Population: 24,000,000

The colours of this flag are derived more directly from those of Marcus Garvey, and are basically those of the ruling party. The shield and crossed spears and white stripes were added at independence in 1963.

▷ **Capital:** Maseru
Population: 1,800,000

This flag was introduced in 1987. The previous flag was adopted on independence in 1966 and was in the colours of the then ruling party. In the present flag the emblem is a stylised version of the coat of arms.

LESOTHO

LIBERIA

◁ **Capital:** Monrovia
Population: 2,500,000

This flag is directly derived from the Stars and Stripes from which freed slaves came to colonise the area. It dates from 27 August 1847 and here the star stands for 'a shining light in the Dark Continent.'

▷ **Capital:** Antananarivo
Population: 11,500,000

Madagascar also has a 'non-political' flag, whose colours recall those of the pre-French kingdom (red and white) with green for the other peoples of the island. It was adopted on 14 October 1958, prior to independence.

MADAGASCAR

MALAWI

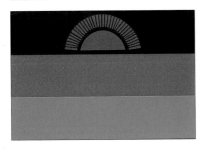

MALI

◁ **Capital:** Lilongwe
Population: 8,500,000
The colours of this flag are derived from the flag of Marcus Garvey. The sun is taken from the coat of arms and expresses the idea of the dawn of a new age. The flag was adopted on independence on 6 July 1964.

▷ **Capital:** Bamako
Population: 8,000,000
Another flag in the Pan-African colours. Originally the flag, when adopted in 1959, had a black outline figure of a man in the centre, and also represented Senegal. The plain tricolour dates from 1 March 1961.

MAURITIUS

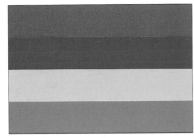

MOZAMBIQUE

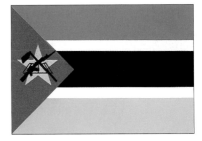

◁ **Capital:** Port Louis
Population: 1,100,000
The flag is a set of stripes in the colours of the coat of arms, although they are sometimes given romantic associations, such as independence (red), the blue of the sea and the light of freedom (yellow).

▷ **Capital:** Maputo
Population: 15,500,000
The colours of this flag were those of FRELIMO, the dominant political party. The design, based on the old party flag, was adopted on 1 May 1983. The devices on the red triangle are a form of the national arms.

NAMIBIA

◁ **Capital:** Windhoek
Population: 1,500,000
The flag was adopted on independence day, 21 March 1990, and is partly based on the colours of SWAPO (blue, red, green). To these have been added white fimbriations to stand for peace, and a gold sun shining in blue sky.

▷ **Capital:** Niamey
Population: 800,000
The flag dates from 23 November 1959. In later times the orange has been interpreted as standing for the Savannah, the white for the river (Niger) and green for the forest. The orange disc represents the sun.

NIGER

NIGERIA

◁ **Capital:** Lagos
Population: 110,000,000
This flag was chosen in a competition, and also has a white band representing the River Niger, in this case flowing through the green land. It has been in use since the day of independence, 1 October 1960.

▷ **Capital:** Kigali
Population: 7,500,000
Another flag in the Pan-African colours. Here the black letter R (for Rwanda) had to be added in order to distinguish the flag from that of Guinea. The flag in this form dates from September 1961.

RWANDA

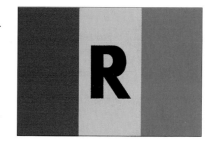

SENEGAL

◁ **Capital:** Dakar
Population: 7,000,000
This flag is derived from that of Mali, to which Senegal was once linked. After splitting from Mali in 1960 Senegal distinguished its flag by adding a green star, taken from its coat of arms, to the centre.

▷ **Capital:** Victoria
Population: 100,000
The flag is based on that of the dominant political party and was adopted when that party seized power in 1977. The party flag had a gold rising sun, and represented the sun rising over the sea.

SEYCHELLES

SIERRA LEONE

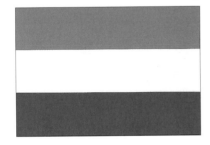

◁ **Capital:** Freetown
Population: 400,000
The colours are heraldic, derived from the coat of arms, which symbolise the 'Lion Mountains' standing above the blue and white of the sea. The flag dates from independence day, 27 April 1961.

▷ **Capital:** Mogadishu
Population: 700,000
The colour and style of the flag recall those of the United Nations, under whose auspices Somalia was administered from 1950-60. The five-pointed star is said to stand for the five countries inhabited by Somalis.

SOMALIA

SOUTH AFRICA

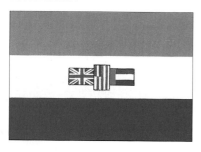

◁ **Capital:** Pretoria
Population: 30,000,000
The colours are derived from those of the Netherlands. In the centre is the flag of the Transvaal, flanked by those of the Orange Free State and the Union Jack. The flag was introduced on 31 May 1928.

▷ **Capital:** Mbabane
Population: 800,000
In the centre of the flag is a Swazi shield and two spears. The field of the flag is derived from one used by Swazi volunteers in World War II. The modern flag was adopted on 30 October 1967, prior to independence.

SWAZILAND

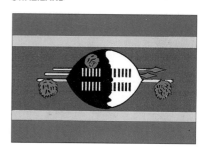

TANZANIA

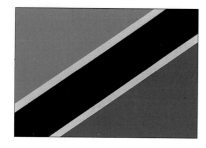

◁ **Capital:** Dodoma
Population: 25,000,000
The flag is a combination of the flags of Tanganyika and Zanzibar, which united in April 1964. The flag of Tanganyika dates from 1961 and was green, black and yellow. The flag of Zanzibar was of blue, black and green.

▷ **Capital:** Lomé
Population: 3,500,000
The flag is in the Pan-African colours and was adopted when the republic became independent on 27 April 1960. The five stripes stand for the five departments of the country, and the star is the 'Star of Hope'.

TOGO

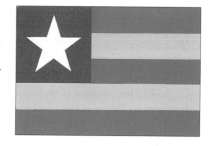

UGANDA

◁ **Capital:** Kampala
Population: 17,000,000
This is another flag based on those of the then dominant political party, the Uganda People's Congress. The emblem is the Great Crested Crane, which was the badge of Uganda in colonial times.

ZAÏRE

▷ **Capital:** Kinshasa
Population: 35,000,000
The flag is in the Pan-African colours, although in a radically new design, based on the flag of the ruling party. It was introduced on 21 November 1971, after the country had used two previous designs.

ZAMBIA

◁ **Capital:** Lusaka
Population: 800,000
This flag was also based on that of the then ruling party, but also has a striking design. The eagle is derived from the former colonial badge of Northern Rhodesia, which also appears in the modern coat of arms.

ZIMBABWE

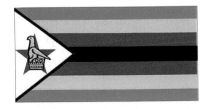

▷ **Capital:** Harare
Population: 9,500,000
This flag is also based on that of the party dominant at independence, with a white section for the minority. The device in the white triangle is the crest from the coat of arms, and includes the Zimbabwe bird.

Index